WEATHER AND CLIMATE

THE POWER OF WEATHER

HOW TIME AND WEATHER CHANGE THE EARTH

by Ellen Labrecque

CAPSTONE PRESS
a capstone imprint

Capstone Captivate is published by Capstone Press, an imprint of Capstone.
1710 Roe Crest Drive, North Mankato, Minnesota, 56003.
www.capstonepub.com

Library of Congress Cataloging-in-Publication Data is available on the Library of
Congress website.
ISBN: 978-1-5435-9155-2 (library binding)
ISBN: 978-1-4966-5777-0 (paperback)
ISBN: 978-1-5435-9160-6 (ebook pdf)

Summary: Describes weathering and erosion caused by wind, water, ice,
and humans.

Image Credits
Dreamstime/Rastislav Bado, 5; iStockphoto/clubfoot, 15; Shutterstock: 4kclips,
25, Amineah, 17, Amit kg, 23, Barbara Ash, cover (tumbleweed), Calin Tatu, cover
(bottom), Dmitry Pichugin, 7, Everett Historical, 12, IgorZh, cover (top), JJ Gouin,
27, Johan Larson, 13, lexaarts, 28, Lisa Parsons, 9, Manun Tapkul, 29, MyImages-
Micha, 6, NASA images, 8, Nicolaj Larsen, 21, Peera_stockfoto, 16, Photoholgic, 22,
Sarah Fields Photography, 24, Tupungato, 20, VOJTa Herout, 18, xbrchx, 19, Yerbolat
Shadrahov, 11

Artistic elements: Shutterstock: gigi rosa, MaddyZ, Rebellion Works, rudall30,

Editorial Credits
Editor: Erika L. Shores; Designer: Tracy McCabe; Media Researcher: Kelly Garvin;
Premedia Specialist: Kathy McColley

Capstone thanks Rachel Humphrey, assistant professor, Department of Atmospheric
and Hydrologic Sciences, St. Cloud State University, St. Cloud, MN, for her expertise
in reviewing this book.

Printed and bound in the USA.
PA99

TABLE OF CONTENTS

Words in **bold** are in the glossary.

CHAPTER 1

EARTH'S MOVERS AND SHAKERS

Imagine spending a day on the beach. In the morning, you build a giant sandcastle. Over the next few hours, the wind blows. It carries away some of your sandcastle. Then people walk by. They step on parts of your castle. They take some of the sand away on their feet. High tide comes. The stronger ocean waves roll over what's left of your castle. The sand goes back out to sea.

What happened to your sandcastle is **erosion**. Erosion is the movement of soil and rock from one place to another. Wind, water, and the actions of people can cause erosion.

FACT

The word "erosion" comes from the Latin word *erosio*. It means to eat away.

Ocean waves erode a sandcastle on the beach.

Weathering and erosion are two processes that help shape the earth. Weathering is the wearing away and breaking down of rock, soil, and sand. Weathering happens through contact with wind, water, air, and humans. Weathering breaks down rock. Erosion moves it to another place. Together these processes carve giant canyons. They wash away beaches and create new ones. They change the shape and size of land.

A stream causes erosion by moving rocks, sand, and soil from one place to another place.

Erosion takes place over thousands or even millions of years. Wind erosion, water erosion, ice erosion, and human erosion have shaped our planet and the way we live on it. These types of erosion will continue to change the earth.

Wind erosion shaped a rocky cliff in the Sahara Desert in Africa.

CHAPTER 2

WIND EROSION

Wind is a powerful force of weathering and erosion. It is especially mighty during storms. Some **hurricane** winds reach speeds of more than 150 miles (240 kilometers) per hour. Forceful gusts speed up erosion.

A weather map shows Hurricane Michael in 2018.

During very strong hurricanes, entire beaches can be washed away in days. In 2018, Hurricane Michael hit Florida. It was so powerful it eroded entire beach towns.

Winds from Hurricane Michael destroyed trees and swept away beaches.

Even when winds aren't powerful, they still carry sand and dirt from one place to another. Winds are constantly changing how the land looks. Wind erosion happens the most in dry places where soil or sand is lighter to carry. It also happens in places where there are not a lot of trees, hills, or mountains. These objects block the wind.

A **desert** is a place that gets little to no rainfall. It is usually flat and doesn't have much plant life to block the wind or hold the soil in place. Sandstorms are a dangerous part of desert life. The whipping sand makes it difficult to see anything. Wind erosion forms piles of sand called **sand dunes**. The highest sand dunes in the world are more than 1,000 feet (305 meters) tall. This is as tall as the Eiffel Tower in Paris, France.

In a sandstorm, wind blows away a great deal of sand in a desert.

FACT

People "surf" down the sides of sand dunes. It is called sandboarding.

Wind erosion occurs especially during **droughts**, or periods of no rain. Soil becomes dry and blows away easily. This happens on farmland where there aren't a lot of trees. Tree roots hold onto water, which helps keep soil moist. Winds don't pick up wet soil as easily as dry soil.

THE DUST BOWL

In the 1930s, a drought called the Dust Bowl struck the middle of the United States. Areas of Kansas and Oklahoma did not have rain for close to 10 years. The dirt became very dry. Wind blew the dusty soil from farmland. There was so much flying dirt that it blocked the sun. The storms were called "black blizzards."

Wind picks up dirt and blows it away in an open field.

CHAPTER 3

WATER EROSION

Water erosion is one of the most powerful forces of weather. It can happen during storms or when too much rain comes at once and the ground isn't able to absorb it all. When rain runs on top of land, it can sometimes take bits of rock and dirt with it. If the land doesn't have many plants to hold the dirt in place, there can be even more erosion.

Heavy rain on a hill or mountain can sometimes cause **landslides**. Landslides happen when soil and rock move quickly down a hillside or mountain all at once. Landslides are dangerous and deadly.

A DEADLY LANDSLIDE

In 1999, one of the worst landslides ever recorded happened. Rain poured down on a mountain range in the country of Venezuela in South America. It caused rocks and mud to tumble down the side. The landslide buried towns at the bottom of the mountains. More than 30,000 people died.

A landslide can carry tons of rock and soil down
a cliff.

Heavy rainfall can sometimes cause rivers and streams to overflow. The water floods over its banks, making the river wider. As the rivers flow, they carry away more rock and dirt. Rivers become deeper and can even change their course.

When rivers flood, they often change the land around them.

Over time, powerful rivers also form canyons. Canyons are steep, narrow **valleys** cut by rivers through rock. The Grand Canyon in Arizona was created by river erosion. The constant **currents** of the Colorado River formed it 5 to 6 million years ago. Today the river is still eroding parts of the canyon.

The Colorado River cuts through the Grand Canyon.

Ocean waves wear away rock and sand. Storms at sea cause big ocean waves to crash onto shorelines. As these waves crash, they bring sand and rocks with them. When the waves go back out, they take away other sand and rocks. Over thousands of years, this water erosion can create rocky cliffs and caves.

Ocean waves change the size and shape of rocks along coastlines.

When the weather is milder, waves are calmer. Calm waves still bring the sand inland, but the sand doesn't go back out to sea as much. This causes new beaches to form. If the sand resettles near the shoreline, **sandbars** form.

A sandbar in the Adriatic Sea near the country of Croatia

CHAPTER 4

ICE EROSION

Glaciers are big sheets of frozen water. They can cause erosion as they move over the ground beneath them. Appearing like large frozen rivers, glaciers form over a long period of time in places with freezing temperatures. Snow piles up. The snow then is pressed down, or compacted, over many years and turns to ice, becoming a glacier.

A glacier in the country of Norway

When glaciers form, they can start to move for many reasons. They might start moving down a slope due to the pull of gravity. These glaciers move down into mountain valleys. Other glaciers flow outward in different directions. They move because their bottoms may not be solid ice. They float on the water beneath them.

Elephant Foot Glacier spreads out after it moves down a valley in the country of Greenland.

When glaciers move, they drag tons of rocks and dirt with them. These rocks and dirt get moved to other places along the path of the glacier. Glaciers also knock giant rocks off nearby land as they travel.

Sometimes a glacier flows between two rocks and continues to move, forcing the rocks farther apart. When this happens, the rocks are worn down, creating more room and changing the rocks' appearance.

It is easy to see how glaciers shaped some mountains. Some mountains have a tall peak called a horn. This horn was shaped over time by two or more glaciers eroding the mountain on three different sides.

Glaciers shaped the Matterhorn. It is part of the Alps mountain range in Europe.

Rocks and soil left behind from a glacier

Glaciers cover about 10 percent of Earth's surface. Most of the glaciers are in Antarctica and Greenland. But about 12,000 years ago, an ice age happened. Big sections of Earth were covered in ice and glaciers. Back then, glaciers helped mold much of our planet by erosion. Glacier erosion made some of the most amazing landforms in the United States, including Yosemite Valley in California and the Great Lakes in the upper Midwest.

Yosemite Valley is in the western United States.

Lake Michigan is one of the five Great Lakes formed by glaciers. The city of Chicago is on the western shore of Lake Michigan.

CHAPTER 5

HUMAN EROSION

Erosion caused by wind, water, and ice is natural. But people cause erosion too. In order to plant new seeds and grow crops, farmers clear fields of other trees and plants. During winter, farm fields remain bare. There is nothing to keep the top layer of dirt in place. Wind and water erode this soil. If too much erosion occurs, the land won't be good enough to farm anymore.

People also cut down trees and clear land to build new homes. Roads and parking lots are developed too. These activities cause erosion. When rain falls, it rushes over the land quickly rather than soaking into it. This causes flooding and landslides.

When water runs quickly over farmland, it erodes soil.

Climate change can also impact erosion. Climate change is a long-term change in Earth's weather. Human activities, such as driving cars and burning coal, can add to climate change by putting more of the gas **carbon dioxide** into the **atmosphere**. When there are higher amounts of carbon dioxide in the air, temperatures rise, which can make glaciers melt faster. The water from the melting glaciers can then cause sea levels to rise, which can cause more erosion along coastlines.

Many factories release carbon dioxide into the air.

Erosion is happening all around us. Sometimes it happens slowly. Other times it happens quickly due to extreme weather. Our land is, and will always be, changing.

A coastline in the country of Thailand shows the effects of erosion.

GLOSSARY

atmosphere (AT-muhss-fihr)—the mixture of gases that surrounds Earth

carbon dioxide (KAHR-buhn dy-AHK-syd)—a gas that has no smell or color

climate (KLY-muht)—the average weather in a place over many years

climate change (KLY-muht CHAYNJ)—a long term change in Earth's climate or weather

current (KUHR-uhnt)—the movement of water in a river or an ocean

desert (DEZ-ert)—a region that receives little to no rainfall

drought (DROUT)—a long period of weather with little or no rainfall

erosion (ee-ROW-zhuhn)—the movement of rock or sand from one place or another by wind, water, ice, and humans

hurricane (HUR-uh-kane)—a strong, swirling wind and rainstorm that starts on the ocean; hurricanes are also called typhoons or cyclones

landslide (LAND-slide)—the downward falling of a mass of dirt, rocks, and earth

sandbar (sand-BAR)—an island of sand formed in a river, stream, or ocean by the water

sand dune (SAND DOON)—a hill of sand formed by the wind

valley (VAL-ee)—a low region surrounded by mountains or hills

weather (WETH-er)—to wear away or break down bigger pieces of rock

READ MORE

Brannon, Cecelia H. *A Look at Erosion and Weathering.* New York: Enslow Publishing, 2016.

Chin, Jason. *Grand Canyon.* New York: Roaring Book Press, 2017.

Hyde, Natalie. *How Do Wind and Water Change Earth?* New York: Crabtree Publishing Company, 2015.

INTERNET SITES

Erosion
https://www.nationalgeographic.org/encyclopedia/erosion/

Erosion!: The Ever-Changing Earth
https://www.kidsdiscover.com/teacherresources/erosion-ever-changing-earth/

The Grand Canyon National Park
https://www.nps.gov/grca/index.htm

INDEX